WINSTON CHURCHILL

Kevin Theakston

SHIRE PUBLICATIONS

Published in Great Britain in 2012 by Shire Publications
Ltd, Midland House, West Way, Botley, Oxford OX2 0PH,
United Kingdom.
44-02 23rd St, Suite 219, Long Island City, NY 11101
E-mail: shire@shirebooks.co.uk   www.shirebooks.co.uk

A CIP catalogue record for this book is available from the
British Library.

Shire Library no. 642   •   ISBN-13: 978 0 74781 045 2

Kevin Theakston has asserted his right under the
Copyright, Designs and Patents Act, 1988, to be identified
as the author of this book.

Designed by Tony Truscott Designs, Sussex, UK
and typeset in Perpetua and Gill Sans.
Printed in China through Worldprint Ltd.

12 13 14 15 16 10 9 8 7 6 5 4 3 2 1

COVER IMAGE
Winston Churchill, with his trademark cigar,
photographed in 1950, a year before he became British
prime minister for the second time.

TITLE PAGE IMAGE
Churchill was sixty-five when he finally became prime
minister in 1940, at a moment of supreme national crisis
and peril. Here he is in Number 10 Downing Street.

CONTENTS PAGE IMAGE
Churchill with the Royal Family on the balcony of
Buckingham Palace on VE Day in May 1945. Two months
later the great 'war winner' was voted out of office in the
first general election held for ten years.

ACKNOWLEDGEMENTS
Bridgeman Art Library / The National Trust, pages 22–3;
Getty Images, page 18; Imagestate.com, page 32; Imperial
War Museum, pages 16, 31 and 34; Mirrorpix, title page
and pages 3, 4, 5, 8, 9, 10, 12, 17, 24, 26, 28, 30, 33, 35,
36, 37, 38, 42, 43, 44 and 45; Mary Evans Picture Library,
cover image and pages 13 and 15; National Portrait
Gallery, pages 5, 20, 21, 40 and 41;
Oldbookillustrations.com, page 6.

Shire Publications is supporting the Woodland Trust, the UK's leading woodland conservation charity, by funding the dedication of trees.

CONTENTS

EARLY LIFE AND ADVENTURES

Blenheim Palace:
ancestral seat
of the Dukes of
Marlborough, one
of the grandest
houses in England,
and Churchill's
birthplace.

WINSTON LEONARD SPENCER CHURCHILL was born on 30 November 1874 at Blenheim Palace in Oxfordshire, the magnificent seat of the Dukes of Marlborough. Churchill was always personally ambitious, self-absorbed and egocentric but he was also always very conscious of his family's place in English history, and of being part of a class that was born to rule and with a tradition of public service. He was proud to be a descendant of the great

soldier-statesman John Churchill, the first Duke of Marlborough (1650–1722).

The most vivid account of the first twenty-five years of Churchill's long life remains his own partial memoir, *My Early Life*, published in 1930. Though inaccurate in places, it is an artful, charming, wise and witty book, part adventure story and part an elegy for the vanished age of aristocratic and imperial rule he had been born into. Some consider it the best of all his books: he had a good story to tell and he told it well. (Later, in 1972, a film, *Young Winston*, was made, based on the book.)

Churchill (in about 1886) with his mother Jennie and younger brother Jack (1880–1947). Churchill adored his American mother, a celebrated society beauty, but she was a fairly remote figure in his childhood.

Born into the Victorian ruling class, Churchill's grandfather (the seventh Duke of Marlborough) was one of Disraeli's ministers and Lord Lieutenant of Ireland, and his father, Lord Randolph Churchill (1849–95), was a controversial Conservative MP and politician. Lord Randolph enjoyed a meteoric rise to power, becoming Chancellor of the Exchequer when he was only thirty-six. But, impulsive, reckless and opportunistic, he committed political suicide with an ill-judged resignation in 1886. He died relatively young (on some accounts from advanced syphilis, on others from a brain tumour). Churchill later wrote a laudatory biography of him, committed to memory huge chunks of his speeches, and was spurred into seeking fame and a political career partly to vindicate his father's reputation and carry forward his political standard. But Churchill never really knew or got close to his father, whom he experienced as remote, chilly and forbidding, and he seems to have been haunted by a sense that his father felt he (Winston) would never measure up or amount to much.

Churchill's mother – Jennie Jerome (1854–1921) – was American and the daughter of a wealthy New York financier. The Marlboroughs were far from rich by ducal standards, and Lord and Lady Randolph lived a profligate, extravagant and debt-ridden style of life; Churchill always knew he would have to make his own fortune.

Churchill hero-worshipped his father, Lord Randolph, a brilliant but self-destructive star of Victorian politics, but they never established a close relationship.

Lady Randolph was a self-indulgent and fashionable society hostess who had many affairs (she was once described as 'having more of the panther than of the woman in her look', and after Lord Randolph died she married twice more, each time to a much younger man). Churchill recalled her as 'beautiful and fascinating', a 'fairy princess'. 'She shone for me like the Evening Star', he wrote. 'I loved her dearly – but at a distance.' Like many upper-class children of that time, Churchill saw little of his parents and he felt neglected. Later (in the 1890s), his relationship with his mother evolved into a useful partnership and she used her social influence to pull strings and to lobby on behalf of her son, to boost his career. But during his childhood, sympathy, love and affection came primarily from his nurse and nanny, Mrs Everest, to whom he became completely devoted and with whom he kept in touch until her death when he was a young man of twenty.

Churchill later described himself as a 'backward schoolboy' and said that his school years were a particularly 'barren and unhappy' period in his life. He certainly got poor school reports, and his wilfulness and unruly behaviour brought frequent beatings. But it is a myth that he was a stupid boy and a dunce at school. It is true that much of the curriculum at Harrow School, where he was in the bottom form, did not interest or engage him – he was hopeless at Greek, Latin and mathematics. However, history, poetry and English literature stirred his imagination, he excelled at essay writing, and he had a prodigious memory. He won a school prize for reciting, without a

At Harrow School, Churchill recalled, 'the subjects which were dearest to the examiners were almost invariably those I fancied least'.

single mistake, 1,200 lines of Macaulay's *Lays of Ancient Rome*. Short and slight, the classic public-school team sports held little appeal for him but he became a champion fencer. Churchill missed out on the normal university experience (at Oxford – where his father had been a student – or Cambridge) of the ruling elite. Much of his real education came later when, as a young army officer, he spent the blisteringly hot afternoons in camp in India reading his way through piles of books on history, philosophy, economics and other subjects, and accounts of parliamentary debates, that he requested his mother to send out to him.

The story is told that Lord Randolph, believing his son not clever enough for university or for a profession like the law, and seeing him playing enthusiastically with his large army of model soldiers, decided that he should have a military career. Even so, he scraped through the exams and got into the Royal Military Academy only on his third attempt and towards the bottom of the entry list; to his father's dismay his marks were too low to qualify him for the infantry but only for the (more expensive) cavalry. But Sandhurst was a new start and gave Churchill the sense of purpose and structure his life had hitherto lacked. He worked hard at his military training, enjoyed the subjects he now studied, and became a good horseman; he passed out with honours, ranked twentieth out of 130 in his class. In February 1895 he was commissioned as a subaltern into the 4th Hussars, a fashionable cavalry regiment.

The young Churchill saw the army as a launch pad for the political career he was already set upon. From the outset he sought what he called 'the swift road to promotion and advancement . . . distinction . . . [and] glamour'. He wanted to make a name for himself – and quickly – and to claim a place on the national political stage, and for that he also needed to make money (MPs not being paid in those days). He was a young man in a hurry (fearing that the Churchills died young) and there was a lot of 'pushing and shoving', as he put it, and energetic exploitation of his and his mother's family and political connections to stretch or circumvent the normal rules and to win him special assignments and postings. He played for his regiment's championship-winning polo team, but humdrum garrison life in India – his regiment was posted to Bangalore – did not appeal to him. A fervent imperialist, he never doubted, however, Britain's right to rule India and was typical of his time in taking white superiority for granted. He struck many contemporaries – including military superiors (such as Kitchener, the head of the army in Egypt) – as bumptious, pushy and self-promoting, a medal-hunter and publicity-seeker. They were right, but he also displayed impressive courage and drive.

Between 1895 and 1900 Churchill took part in or witnessed military action in Cuba, India's wild north-west frontier region, the Sudan and South

Churchill as a subaltern in India, where his regiment, the 4th Hussars, was sent in 1896.

Africa. It was while reporting for the press on the Spanish campaign against guerrilla rebels in Cuba that he developed his life-long taste for Havana cigars and for siestas (breaking the day into two with an afternoon nap, he would always later insist, recharged his energies and actually increased his working hours and capacity). There could be no doubting his physical bravery, whether in vicious skirmishes with Afghan tribesmen, taking part (with the 21st Lancers) in the last great cavalry charge of the British army at the battle of Omdurman, or under Boer rifle and artillery fire on the South African veldt. He was mentioned in despatches. There were many near misses and close calls ('there is nothing more exhilarating than to be shot at without result', he later said), and he himself shot and killed other human beings. He clearly relished danger and found war exciting but he was also profoundly aware – and at first hand – of its squalor, horror and tragedy.

Churchill combined being a junior officer with being a war correspondent, writing about the campaigns he took part in for newspapers and also publishing books about them: *The Story of the Malakand Field Force* (1898), *The River War* (1899), *London to Ladysmith via Pretoria* (1900), *Ian Hamilton's March* (1900). These showed literary talent, and were well received and commercially successful. At the time of the Boer War, writing for the *Morning Post*, he was actually the highest-paid war correspondent of the time. Nor did he flinch from criticising military strategy and the decisions and mistakes of the generals. He also tried his hand at a novel, *Savrola* (1900), a rather melodramatic book usually described as a 'Ruritanian romance'.

The breakthrough event that really sealed his personal fame came about after his capture by the Boers in November 1899, when an armoured train he was travelling on with a detachment of soldiers was derailed and ambushed. Although technically by then no longer a serving regular soldier but a journalist (he had formally resigned his commission earlier that year), he was in the thick of the action and was taken prisoner. But his dramatic escape from imprisonment in Pretoria – the Boers offering a £25 'dead or alive' reward for his recapture – catapulted him onto the front pages and made him a household name at a time when good news stories about the South African war were in short supply.

It was as a young officer in India that Churchill started to predict to people that one day he would become prime minister. He made his first speech on a political platform – at a Conservative Party 'Primrose League' meeting in Bath – while home on leave in 1897. Two years later he was invited to stand for the Conservatives in a by-election in the predominantly working-class mill town of Oldham in Lancashire, but was defeated. He stood again in Oldham in the October 1900 general election – known as the 'khaki election' as the Conservative government sought to benefit from the patriotic enthusiasm aroused by the Boer War and to exploit Liberal divisions over the war – and, this time, he was narrowly elected (by a margin of only 222 votes). After embarking on a moneymaking British and North American lecture tour about his South African adventures, he took his seat in the House of Commons on 14 February 1901 – an institution in which he was to spend virtually all the rest of his life serving.

Churchill's triumphant welcome in Durban in December 1899 after escaping from a Boer prisoner of war camp – almost overnight he found himself a national hero.

9

THE RISING (AND FALLING) POLITICIAN

'POLITICS are almost as exciting as war, and quite as dangerous', Churchill once said. 'In war you can be only killed once, but in politics many times.' Few politicians have had in this sense as many 'lives' as Churchill, his career being a story of advances, setbacks, successes and disasters. He had been written off as politically finished several times before he finally reached the top. Had he died in or before 1939, it has been argued, he would have been seen, overall, as a political failure.

Certainly the first half of his political career had an amazing 'snakes and ladders' character. Symptomatic of this were his electoral ups and downs and his lack of a secure constituency base. He had to move from Oldham, where he had scraped in in 1900, to Manchester North West in 1906 only to lose that seat in 1908 (after the by-election then obligatory for newly appointed Cabinet ministers), moving to Dundee, from which he was later evicted by the local voters in 1922. He then fought two unsuccessful by-elections in 1923 and 1924 before being found a safe seat in Epping (later renamed Woodford) on the outskirts of London. In party terms he was also footloose, beginning as a Conservative, becoming a Liberal, returning to the Conservatives, and often hankering after political realignments or an all-party or coalition government – not surprisingly, many thought he was really an unprincipled careerist.

As a young politician-on-the-make Churchill was extraordinarily ambitious, energetic and thrusting. But despite his undoubted abilities as a speaker (at which he worked very hard, putting in long hours of detailed preparation) and in ministerial office, he aroused widespread distrust, often being seen as impulsive, opportunistic, lacking in judgement, reckless, brash, bumptious and unreliable. He had few political friends, annoyed and discomforted people high and low right across the political spectrum, and was never a 'safe party man'. This pattern was established from the very start of his parliamentary career when he was a rebellious and trouble-making Conservative MP. He called himself a 'Tory Democrat' (claiming to follow in his father's footsteps – and he went on to write a biography of Lord

Opposite:
Churchill speaking from the top of a car in Manchester as a young Cabinet minister in April 1908.

Churchill in about 1900: driven, pushy and ambitious; elected as a Member of Parliament aged just twenty-five.

Opposite: Churchill as First Lord of the Admiralty in 1914, discussing naval strategy with Admiral Sir John Jellicoe, commander of the Grand Fleet, and Admiral Sir Charles Madden.

Randolph, published in 1906), attacked proposed army reforms and the level of War Office expenditure, and was a prominent member of a group of backbench gadflies and rebels called the 'Hooligans' (or 'Hughligans', after their leader, Lord Hugh Cecil). As the Conservative Party and Arthur Balfour's government tore itself apart over the issue of tariffs and protectionism, Churchill – a free-trader who opposed food taxes – found himself even more at odds with his own party and its leadership. His constituency association passed a vote of no confidence in him, the Conservative whip was withdrawn, and in May 1904 he crossed the floor of the House and switched parties, sitting as a Liberal.

Churchill enjoyed a meteoric rise through the ranks as a Liberal before the First World War. Appointed as a parliamentary under- secretary (a junior minister) at the Colonial Office after the Liberals' 1906 landslide election victory, he was then promoted to become President of the Board of Trade in 1908 (aged just thirty-three he was the youngest Cabinet minister since 1866), moving on to be Home Secretary (1910–11) and then First Lord of the Admiralty (1911–15). He enjoyed and relished office and power, and thrived on the pressures of high politics. (Later, deprived of ministerial office and 'intense executive activities', he said that he felt like 'a sea-beast fished up from the depths, or a diver too suddenly hoisted.') But he was a difficult subordinate, a difficult colleague and a difficult boss. 'Once a week or oftener Mr Churchill came to the office bringing with him some adventurous or impossible projects', a senior civil servant of the time recalled. 'But after half an hour's discussion something was evolved which was still adventurous but not impossible.' Fellow Cabinet ministers frequently resented his pushiness and the way he would interfere in their areas of responsibility. Asquith, the prime minister after 1908, backed him, promoted him, found him useful and sometimes amusing, but was also wary and conscious of the negatives and the downside of Churchill's super-charged political personality.

He got things done, however, and had many achievements to his name in this period. At the Colonial Office he had been much involved in South African issues, including the restoration of self-government and the framing of new constitutions for the Transvaal and the Orange Free State. After 1908 he became a political ally of Lloyd George, the fiery Welsh radical and

AUGUST 15, 1914]　　　　　*THE SPHERE*　　　　　183

The MEN who are DIRECTING BRITAIN'S NAVY.

DRAWN BY F. MATANIA

THE FIRST LORD WITH HIS TWO HIGHEST EXECUTIVE OFFICERS

RIGHT HON. WINSTON CHURCHILL—Mr. Churchill is not quite forty years old yet, but he is known throughout the world as a most capable administrator of English affairs. He was first elected for Parliament in 1900 as a Conservative member, but in the year 1906 he was returned for N.W. Manchester as a Liberal. He has been First Lord of the Admiralty since 1911

REAR-ADMIRAL CHARLES MADDEN (second in command) has just relinquished the command of the 3rd Cruiser Squadron of the Home Fleets. He entered the Navy in 1875. He was in command of one of the earliest flotillas of torpedo-boat destroyers in the Mediterranean. He became captain of the original "Dreadnought" in 1907. He has gained a high reputation

ADMIRAL SIR JOHN JELLICOE—Vice-Admiral Jellicoe has just been appointed Commander-in-Chief of the Home Fleet in place of Admiral Callaghan. Admiral Jellicoe has acted since 1912 as Second Sea Lord of the Admiralty. He saw service in China from 1898-1901, when he commanded the Naval Brigade there. He was commander of the Atlantic Fleet during 1910-11

Chancellor of the Exchequer, the two men becoming central instigators of, and the force behind, the Liberal government's landmark social welfare reforms. Lloyd George was the dominant figure but Churchill was responsible at the Board of Trade for the creation of labour exchanges, the introduction of minimum wages for the so-called 'sweated trades', and proposals for unemployment insurance. He was a reform-minded Home Secretary, wanting to reduce the number of petty criminals sent to jail and to reform prisons; in that office he also introduced legislation to improve safety in the coal mines and a bill to regulate the hours and working conditions of shop workers. At the Admiralty he imposed his authority over obstructive admirals and pushed through important modernizing reforms, creating a Naval War Staff, introducing a new class of fast battleships, promoting the development of submarines and naval air power (himself taking flying lessons, sometimes dicing with death in the process), improving sailors' pay and conditions, and seeing through the conversion from coal to oil-fired engines, negotiating the purchase of 51 per cent of the shares of the Anglo-Persian Oil Company to secure supplies of oil.

Wherever he went there was political trouble and fireworks. While Conservatives hated him as a turncoat and traitor, many Liberals were doubtful he was really one of them. He was well to the fore in the great political and constitutional battles over the 'People's Budget' and reform of the House of Lords in the 1909–11 period, attacking the Lords as antiquated and reactionary. The vehemence of the aristocrat-turned-radical further fuelled Tory hatred of him, but Churchill did not believe in completely overturning the social and economic order and his radical phase was brief. He was a paternalistic reformer, championing the cause of 'the left-out millions', but not an egalitarian, and was an opponent of socialism who believed in 'levelling up' and a welfare safety-net, not in the abolition of capitalism. He was opposed to votes for women and became a target for militant suffragettes. His tough-minded response as Home Secretary to strikes in the Welsh pits and on the railways won him the enmity of the labour movement (though it is a myth that he sent troops to shoot striking miners at Tonypandy in Wales). Further controversy was aroused by his interventions in the Irish question, which heated up spectacularly in the years before 1914. Churchill supported Home Rule and a Dublin parliament, while proposing an opt-out or exclusion for Protestant Ulster, combining tub-thumping platform-speech belligerence and behind-the-scenes attempts at conciliation. The situation was too charged for a compromise to be reached, however, and (as the Ulster crisis intensified in early 1914) his move of a naval battle squadron close to Belfast was seen as provocative and threatening – another thing his Conservative enemies would not forgive or forget.

In the midst of all this political strife and striving, Churchill had married in September 1908 and was soon the father of a growing family (five children

being born between 1909 and 1922, of whom one – a daughter, Marigold, born in 1918 – tragically died in 1921). To his credit, and unlike some of his class, relatives and political colleagues, he married for love not money, and was entirely faithful throughout his married life. Clementine Churchill's mother, Lady Blanche Hozier, was the daughter of a Scottish peer and was separated from her husband (who was almost certainly not Clementine's actual father). Brought up in rather straitened circumstances, Clementine (1885–1977) was beautiful, charming and intelligent. Their marriage was not always an easy one, however, for they had dissimilar characters, temperaments and styles of life, and Churchill's free-spending habits, his drinking and his gambling troubled her. Nor did she approve of his more raffish friends and cronies, particularly disliking F. E. Smith, Lord Beaverbrook and Brendan Bracken. The strains and anxieties of their life sometimes badly affected her health and nerves. But, for all the ups and downs, it was a close, affectionate and enduring marriage, as their extensive correspondence – with their pet names for each other: 'Kat' or 'Cat' for Clementine, 'Pig' or 'Pug' for Winston – shows. Clementine provided and held together a secure and supportive domestic environment for Churchill. She was herself a good judge of people (often a better one than her politician-husband) and was politically quite astute – Churchill often sought her advice and would have benefitted from following it more often than he did. She had a mind of her own and always remained at heart a Liberal, disliking the Conservative Party her husband eventually came to lead. (In her old age,

Winston Churchill and Clementine Hozier, photographed in 1908 on the occasion of their engagement. Theirs was a long and close marriage, but with its ups and downs. Once after a row Clementine burst out, 'Winston, I have been married to you for 45 years for better' – then, loudly – 'AND FOR WORSE!'

Soldiers going over the top at Cape Helles, Gallipoli, in June 1915. The disasters of the Dardanelles operation and the Gallipoli campaign nearly wrecked Churchill's political career for good.

when she was made a peer after Churchill had died, she sat in the House of Lords on the cross-benches.)

Churchill was lucky to survive the First World War – both politically and personally. He had been one of the leading figures in a divided Liberal Cabinet to support British involvement in the war. He then showed great energy, dynamism and vision as a wartime minister, brimming with ideas (often unwelcome to the military top brass and to his political colleagues) about strategy and military operations, and championing the unorthodox and the innovative – lending crucial support, for instance, to the development of the early tanks (or 'landships'). Faced with the stalemate and slaughter of the western front, he asked: 'Are there not other alternatives to sending our armies to chew barbed wire in Flanders?' But his political career was almost wrecked by him being made the scapegoat for the disasters of the Dardanelles campaign – the failed attempt to capture Constantinople, knock Turkey out of the war, aid Russia and put pressure on Germany's eastern front. Churchill had certainly been the leading advocate of the operation but the War Cabinet approved it and he could not be blamed for all the mistakes made during the Gallipoli campaign (during which his younger brother, Jack Churchill, a major in the army, served as a staff officer). Nevertheless his enemies seized on the opportunity and when a coalition government was formed under Asquith in May 1915, the Conservatives insisted that he be moved out of his position at the Admiralty and he was shunted into the non-job of Chancellor of the Duchy of Lancaster for a few months before he resigned in frustration and left the government in November 1915. It was one of the bleakest moments of his life.

For six months (November 1915 to May 1916) Churchill served on the front line with the army in France. He remained a Member of Parliament during this period (and spoke powerfully in the Commons when home on leave). Back in October 1914 he had personally rallied and directed the defence of Antwerp, holding up the German advance along the Channel coast for several crucial days, sending a telegram to the Cabinet offering to resign as a minister and take up a military command – something that provoked disbelief and laughter from his fellow ministers. His political career now apparently in ruins, he hoped to be given command of a brigade but that was vetoed and, after serving for a month with the Grenadier Guards, he was put in charge of the 6th Battalion Royal Scots Fusiliers as a lieutenant colonel, serving in the trenches at Ploegsteert ('Plugstreet'). He was an inspiring and effective, if unconventional, commanding officer. In all twenty-two Members of Parliament were killed in action while serving in uniform during the First World War. Churchill was fortunate not to be among their number – he came under fire while on patrols out in no-man's-land and on one occasion his dugout was destroyed by a shell, killing a soldier, only minutes after he had left it.

After his battalion was merged with another in a regimental reorganization, Churchill returned to parliamentary politics in the summer

Churchill in army uniform, wearing a French steel helmet, serving on the front line in the First World War.

of 1916. But he had to wait until July 1917 before getting behind a ministerial desk again, when Lloyd George (who had taken over as prime minister in December 1916) braved opposition from the Conservatives and brought back Churchill as Minister of Munitions. Churchill went on to serve until October 1922 in Lloyd George's coalition government, becoming Minister for War and Air in late 1918 and then Colonial Secretary in 1921. At one point he angled for the creation of a Minister of Defence, doubtless looking forward to filling the post himself and lording it over the army, navy and the air force (he gave important support to the existence of the RAF as a separate armed service at this time), but the idea was blocked.

The Liberal Party had been split down the middle by the ousting of Asquith in 1916 and while Churchill remained nominally a Liberal, on Lloyd George's side of the party, his political instincts and identity now seemed

Portrait of Churchill (1916) by Sir John Lavery, the famous celebrity portrait painter and friend of Churchill's, whose wife, Hazel, herself an artist, taught Churchill how to paint.

more right wing. One reason for this was his strong and vocal anti-Bolshevism after Lenin and the communists had seized power in Russia. Churchill absolutely detested communism and believed that the dangers of an evil and tyrannical 'red peril' were so great that the victorious allies should make a magnanimous peace with the defeated Germany for the sake of European security. He would have liked to go very much further in intervening to help the Russian 'Whites' fighting against the Bolsheviks than a reluctant British Cabinet and a war-weary public would support. At home he increasingly seemed the labour movement's enemy, with the trade unions and the Labour Party growing in strength after 1918 but being denounced by him as extreme and unfit to govern.

Just as before the war, he continued to play a leading role in Irish affairs. As War Secretary he backed tough action, including the deployment of the 'Black and Tans', a counter-insurgency force fighting terrorism with terror, against Sinn Fein and the IRA. But then he played an important part in the negotiation of a settlement in Ireland in 1921 that saw the creation of the Irish Free State (and partition, with the six counties of Ulster remaining part of the UK), striking up a rapport with Michael Collins, the Irish revolutionary leader who was later killed during the Irish civil war. As Colonial Secretary he also played a part in reshaping the Middle East after the war and the collapse of the Ottoman Empire, appointing Lawrence of Arabia (T. E. Lawrence) his adviser on Arab affairs and grappling with the problems of Mesopotamia (Iraq), Palestine and Transjordan. Churchill was sympathetic to Zionism but insisted that a 'Jewish national home' should not extend east of the River Jordan.

By the time Lloyd George fell from power in October 1922, Churchill had rebuilt his political career after his wartime nadir. But he then faced a new challenge, or rather two challenges. One was to find a parliamentary seat again after his election defeat at Dundee – the political train always moves quickly on and he wanted and needed to get back on it as soon as possible. The second problem was to find a political home as party politics shifted, with the Liberals being driven into third place and the Conservative–Labour divide coming to define the battleground of politics. 'Ratting' and then 're-ratting' might cause embarrassment for some politicians but Churchill had a thick skin and his next move could only ever be to return to the party he had left in 1904. He finally broke with the Liberals after they put a minority Labour government into office in January 1924, when the general election produced a hung parliament. After standing as an 'Independent Anti-Socialist' in a by-election in March 1924 he was then adopted as a 'Constitutionalist' candidate by the local association in the safe Conservative seat of Epping, returning to parliament after the general election of October 1924.

POLITICAL TROUBLES AND DARKENING CLOUDS

Bᴇᴛᴡᴇᴇɴ 1900 and 1922 Churchill had spent fifteen years in ministerial office; years of excitement, controversy and much achievement. Between 1922 and the outbreak of war in 1939 he spent less than five years in government office. The 1920s and 1930s were a no less controversial period in his career, but the latter decade in particular was a period of political frustration and failure; only the outbreak of war in 1939 allowed him another political comeback.

When the Conservatives returned to office in 1924 prime minister Stanley Baldwin – recognising that many Conservatives still disliked and distrusted Churchill, but probably feeling that such a powerful but often wayward political heavyweight was safer inside rather than outside the tent – astonished many people by catapulting Churchill back into the centre of power, appointing him to be Chancellor of the Exchequer. He was proud to hold his father's old post and loved making a splash on budget day (he presented five budgets from 1924 to 1929). But, knowing little about the problems of economic policy and the technicalities of finance, it was not necessarily a post he was suited for. In regard to one of the biggest issues of his chancellorship – the ill-fated decision to return to the Gold Standard in 1925 at the pre-war rate of $4.86 to the pound – he was unable and unwilling to resist the combined weight of Treasury officials, the Bank of England, the financial establishment and the political conventional wisdom of the time, though he was warned of the dangers and the problems of an over-valued currency by some outside experts like the economist John

Maynard Keynes. Churchill had some doubts and said he would rather see 'finance less proud and industry more content', complaining that the Bank of England seemed 'perfectly happy in the spectacle of Britain possessing the finest credit in the world simultaneously with a million and a quarter unemployed'. But in the end he was convinced the decision was necessary. The effects on struggling export industries were damaging, however, and it put pressure on jobs and wages, Churchill later regarding it as one of his greatest blunders.

During the General Strike of 1926 – when millions of workers came out in support of the miners, who were locked in a bitter dispute with the coal owners – Churchill seemed a militaristic hawk. He talked wildly about being prepared to call in the army, wanted to commandeer the BBC to broadcast government propaganda, and used *The British Gazette* – a government news-sheet he was put in charge of – to rail against the strike as a challenge to democracy and the constitution, describing striking workers as 'the enemy'. This reinforced organised labour's distrust of him, something that lasted until after the outbreak of the Second World War. Once the Trade Union Congress had called off the strike after nine days, however, he was prepared to negotiate with the miners and took a relatively conciliatory line to try and resolve their dispute, but was overruled by hardliners in the Cabinet.

Punch cartoon of 1924, 'The Prodigal's return', on Churchill going back to the Conservative Party. 'Anyone can rat', he said himself, 'but it takes a certain amount of ingenuity to re-rat.'

Churchill once likened Treasury officials to 'inverted Micawbers, waiting for something to turn down.' But as Chancellor he took a tough line himself on defence spending, fighting Cabinet battles to resist plans for the expansion of the navy and the RAF (earlier in his career, of course, he had been a champion of both services – now he was 'economy mad', complained the First Sea Lord). At his insistence the 'Ten Year Rule' was put on a permanent rolling basis – financial plans for the armed services would be based on the assumption that there would be no war for the next ten years unless a new serious threat emerged. There was not the 'slightest chance' of a war with Japan 'in our lifetime', he told Baldwin. It was ironic that the weaknesses in British defence capabilities that Churchill was to criticise so strongly in the 1930s could in part be traced back to decisions made when he had control of the national purse-strings.

Churchill crammed much else besides politics into his life in these years. His appetite for life was immense. He played his last game of polo in 1927

Next page: Chartwell, Kent: Churchill's beloved country house, his base and his home between 1922 and 1964.

Churchill did not take up painting until he was forty, but it then became an absorbing passion for the rest of his life.

when he was in his early fifties but still enjoyed riding and hunting. He had taken up painting in 1915 and it became a major passion of his, his easel and paints always accompanying him on his holidays and travels abroad. Painting gave him a release from the stresses of political life and helped him cope with his depressions. It was one of the few things he did that absorbed him so much he would stop talking. 'If it weren't for painting', he once reportedly said, 'I couldn't live; I couldn't bear the strain of things.' He was a talented amateur, loving bright colours, excelling at landscapes and still lifes, and painting hundreds of canvases over his lifetime (but just one during the Second World War – a picture of Marrakesh, which he presented to President Roosevelt). He even exhibited at the Royal Academy, being made an Honorary Academician Extraordinary.

Meanwhile, his literary output – in the form of books, newspaper and magazine articles – was prodigious. He worked with amazing speed and energy, building on the work of research assistants and dictating huge chunks of prose to relays of secretaries. Between 1923 and 1931 he published a massive six-volume history of the First World War. 'Winston has written a big book about himself and called it *The World Crisis*', was the droll comment of one politician. It is true that Churchill did justify his own actions and decisions, particularly in relation to Gallipoli and his time at the Admiralty. But the books were very readable and successful, making him a great deal of money. The autobiographical *My Early Life* was published in 1930, and two volumes of essays, *Thoughts and Adventures* and *Great Contemporaries*, appeared in 1932 and 1937 respectively. Churchill would turn from writing about 'parliamentary government and the economic problem', to pen a piece on Marshall Foch, George V or George Bernard Shaw, and then write an essay about Moses. He showed his talent for writing military history in his four-volume biography of his great ancestor the Duke of Marlborough, which appeared between 1933 and 1938. While Churchill was researching Marlborough's battlefields in 1932 one of Hitler's circle tried unsuccessfully to set up a meeting between the two men in Munich – they never did meet (though Churchill did meet Mussolini in the 1920s and was for some time impressed by the Italian dictator). In the last couple of years before the outbreak of war in 1939 a multi-volume *History of the English-Speaking Peoples* was started. His articles for British and American newspapers and magazines were widely syndicated. He produced, in all, millions of words and, it has been calculated, Churchill was probably the highest-paid English writer of his day.

Churchill once said he lived 'from hand to mouth' – and he needed the money he earned from his writing (and from lecture tours) to support his extravagant lifestyle. Winston 'is a man of simple tastes', his friend F. E. Smith once said. 'He is prepared to put up with the best of everything.' Excellent food and drink he took for granted. He was undoubtedly dependent on alcohol: 'life would not be worth living' he replied when once challenged, for a wager, to renounce it for a year. 'I have taken more out of alcohol than alcohol has taken out of me', he insisted. He lost a lot of money in the 1929 Wall Street Crash and his beloved country house in Kent, Chartwell Manor, together with his servants and staff, cost a huge amount to run. Churchill had bought Chartwell in the early 1920s without telling his wife – who disliked it – and poured a fortune into its renovation and development. It became his home and a political base. He enjoyed landscaping its grounds and he even took up bricklaying, building many of the walls in the grounds and building a cottage on his new property.

There was no place for Churchill in the Conservative-dominated 'National' governments of the 1930s (under prime ministers MacDonald, Baldwin and then Chamberlain). Churchill's political isolation in these 'wilderness years' was, to a large extent, self-inflicted – the result of taking up causes that put him at odds with his party leadership and mainstream political opinion, and surrounding himself with a small coterie of friends and cronies (some with doubtful reputations) rather than building wide support among the steady party loyalists on the backbenches. He came to seem something of a political has-been. On the big domestic issues of the day, such as unemployment, he had little to say. And on the issues he did speak out on he often seemed extreme, reactionary or quixotic.

Bricklaying at Chartwell. 'I have had a delightful month', he once confessed in the late 1920s, 'building a cottage and dictating a book: two hundred bricks and two thousand words a day.'

After the Conservatives lost the 1929 general election and went into opposition, he resigned from the Shadow Cabinet in January 1931 over policy towards India. The Conservatives supported bi-partisan plans to grant limited self-government and dominion status for India. But supported by a group of right-wing 'die-hard' Conservative MPs, and with strong support among the Tory grass roots, Churchill controversially (and in the end unsuccessfully) fought the proposals and associated legislation in a violent, tooth-and-nail campaign that went on until 1935. His language was often wild – comparing Gandhi to Hitler, for instance, predicting a dire future for a self-governing India, and arguing that the end of the Raj would be fatal for British power in the world and threaten living standards at home. Some suspected Churchill was using the India issue to try to replace Baldwin as leader but it was his own reputation and standing that suffered.

Churchill's judgement was called into question again in December 1936 during the abdication crisis when – affected by his friendship with Edward VIII and by his romantic view of monarchy – he ended up on the wrong side of the collision between the new king and the government, parliament and the political establishment. He pleaded for Edward to be given more time, in the hope that his mistress, Mrs Simpson, would disappear from the scene or the idea of him marrying her could be abandoned, avoiding a constitutional crisis. But his enemies suspected (wrongly) that he was manoeuvring to become the potential leader of a 'king's party' leading a 'royalist' government if Baldwin resigned because the king would not take his ministers' advice. Churchill was stunned to find himself howled down in the House of Commons when he tried to speak up for the king, left more isolated and discredited than ever, and many now felt that his career was ruined.

If Churchill had not run down his political capital so much with his interventions on India and on the side of Edward VIII, his warnings about Hitler, Nazi Germany and the need for Britain to rearm might have commanded more support than they did at the time. While he was clear about the menace and the deadly threat posed by Hitler's Germany, Churchill tended to neglect or downplay other international dangers or aggression from fascist powers or dictatorial regimes in the 1930s – by Japan in the Far East or by Mussolini's Italy – and he did not disagree with the government over the policy of non-intervention in the Spanish civil war. It should not be forgotten that the policy of appeasement had widespread public support – as seen at the time of the Munich settlement in the autumn of 1938, in the wave of national relief at the prospect of war being averted. Churchill was in a minority in calling Munich 'a total and unmitigated defeat'. Only as Hitler's appetite came to be seen as insatiable and as he broke his promises did the national mood shift.

Nor was Churchill the sort of lonely 'prophet' or outsider of the later mythology. He was drawn into Whitehall deliberations by being made a member of the Air Defence Committee, and he was helped by data and briefings supplied to him, in contravention of the rules about official secrecy, by disaffected officials in the intelligence service, the RAF and the Foreign Office, which he used in his powerful parliamentary speeches. Moreover it may be, as some historians suggest, that the government did not mind being attacked so much by Churchill because it helped it appear moderate – Churchill was a warmonger, ministers could say, but not them. In any case the real arguments were about the scale and pace and nature of rearmament, and the government did more than later critics often gave it credit for, particularly in building up air power and air defences. Churchill was not infallible: he (and others) over-estimated the real strength of the German *Luftwaffe*; he under-estimated the threat posed by submarines and the vulnerability of surface warships to air-attack; he did not favour building up the sort of large army that was eventually needed to wage war against Germany; and he put too much faith in the strength of the French army.

In the end, however, it was Churchill's isolation in the 1930s as a Cassandra-type figure warning about what he called 'the gathering storm', and the fact that he could avoid the taint of association with the failings of the Conservatives, that opened the way for him to return to power. As war loomed in the spring and summer of 1939, and opinion turned against appeasement, his standing with the public and in the press rose. Chamberlain, however, resisted his inclusion in the government until the outbreak of war made it unavoidable, and he was then appointed First Lord of the Admiralty – the job he had held twenty-five years earlier at the start of the First World War. A signal was flashed around the navy: 'Winston is back'.

'FINEST HOUR'

THE SECOND WORLD WAR is universally seen as the climax of Churchill's career, and he is usually described as the prime minister who won the war. But it is worth remembering that he was not actually British prime minister when war broke out with Germany's invasion of Poland, only joining Chamberlain's government when Britain declared war on Germany two days later on 3 September 1939 and not himself becoming PM until 10 May 1940. And nor was he in power when the war finally ended with Japan's surrender on 15 August 1945, having decisively lost the general election and resigned office on 26 July (the war in Europe having ended with the German surrender on 8 May). In a more fundamental sense, it would be more accurate to say that, rather than 'winning' the war, Churchill's real contribution had been to avoid defeat and to keep Britain in the war in the dark days of 1940–41. Winning the war and defeating Germany and Japan took the military might and power of Russia and the United States. Long before the end of the war Churchill was painfully aware of Britain's limited means compared to these two behemoths, and gloomy about what that meant for her power and place in the post-war world.

Churchill was characteristically energetic and dynamic as First Lord of the Admiralty and a member of the War Cabinet in 1939 and 1940, constantly pressing for offensive action and impatient with the so-called 'phoney war' (when there were no major military operations on the continent of Europe). He urged various schemes to prosecute the war more aggressively – dropping mines into the River Rhine, sending a naval force into the Baltic, mining Norwegian waters to block the transportation of Swedish iron ore to Germany, sending troops to the north of Norway – but military advisers were sceptical and other ministers cautious and prevaricating. However, no sooner had the Cabinet finally agreed to Churchill's plan to lay mines off the Norwegian coast and occupy Narvik when the Germans pre-empted allied action, and invaded Denmark and Norway in April 1940, swiftly brushing aside and forcing the withdrawal of British forces. The muddle, incompetence and confusions of the Norway campaign, ending in an ignominious

Opposite:
The prime minister visiting a bomb- damaged site in London (1944) after a German 'flying bomb' attack.

The outbreak of the Second World War: *Daily Mirror* front page (4 September 1939) announcing Churchill's return to high office after ten years in the political wilderness.

evacuation, seemed like another Gallipoli. But whereas that earlier disaster had derailed (and almost wrecked) Churchill's political career, this new one – for which he certainly bore a share of the responsibility – actually propelled him into the premiership.

In a dramatic parliamentary debate (7–8 May 1940) on the Norway campaign – in which Churchill put up a strong defence of the government – there was fierce criticism of prime minister Chamberlain and, when the vote was taken, the government's normal majority was massively reduced by a backbench rebellion. Everyone recognized a new coalition government would have to be formed. Chamberlain clung on to the bitter end, even trying to use the breaking news of the start of the big German offensive in the west on 10 May to delay the inevitable. But the Labour Party delivered the *coup-de-grace* by making it clear that they would enter government only under another prime minister. Churchill was not Chamberlain's first choice as his successor, and nor did ruling 'Establishment' circles, the King, or the bulk of Conservative MPs want him. They would have preferred the Foreign Secretary, Lord Halifax, but at the crucial moment Halifax lacked the stomach to seize the ultimate prize and ruled himself out. Churchill's moment had finally come. 'I felt as if I were walking with destiny,' he later wrote, 'and all my past life had been but a preparation for this hour and for this trial . . . I was sure I would not fail.'

Churchill was not the leader of the majority party in the House of Commons when he became prime minister. Chamberlain remained Conservative Party leader and sat in the small War Cabinet until he resigned due to ill health in October 1940 (dying a month later). Only then did Churchill become party leader but many Tories could not forget his past and continued to doubt his commitment to the interests of their party. He headed an all-party coalition – a genuinely national government – with Labour politicians in senior ministerial posts, including Clement Attlee the Labour leader as deputy prime minister, some Liberals in office, and a range of non-party technocrats, businessmen and administrators given important ministerial assignments too. While a powerful, resolute and dominating prime minister, Churchill always sought to maintain the principle and the reality of collective responsibility, carrying his Cabinet colleagues with him. Although there were few big issues on which he was overruled by his colleagues during the war, this was not because he was a dictator – Roosevelt and Stalin, he once said, 'could order; I had to convince and persuade.'

What sort of prime minister was he? While often portrayed as operating in a hugely personal, informal and idiosyncratic manner that would be given poor marks by any management studies handbook, some of his organisational arrangements were actually highly effective. Churchill had witnessed Lloyd George's failure to control the generals in the First World War, and as prime minister he was determined to gather the reins of control into his hands and establish civilian control over the military. No British prime minister has been so involved in supervising military strategy and defence decision-making as was Churchill. (Equally, he is the only one to have worn military uniform(s) in office, as innumerable wartime photographs show.) He appointed himself Minister of Defence, set up a Defence Committee of the Cabinet and a personal military secretariat, and dealt directly with the chiefs of staff through staff conferences. He had plenty of tough arguments with them, and a sometimes stormy relationship with the Chief of the Imperial General Staff (from 1941) and his foremost military adviser, General Sir Alan Brooke, who would stand up to him and argue back, and who managed to deflect him from some of his crazier schemes. But he never overruled the chiefs of staff on a purely military matter.

Whereas a peacetime British Cabinet usually has between twenty and twenty-five ministers, Churchill's wartime War Cabinet varied in size between five and eight minsters, with an underpinning structure of committees dealing with particular areas of policy or tricky issues. Churchill always had a pronounced animus against committees, feeling that they usually involved much passing of the buck, evasion of responsibility, wasted time and blurred decision-making, and that they proliferated endlessly (Whitehall, he used to complain, was in danger of being overrun with committees as Australia was with rabbits). Although he had his suspicions of the civil service

The underground room in which the War Cabinet would meet during the Second World War. As prime minister, Churchill would sit in the seat in front of the wall map.

World War Two poster depicting Churchill as a John Bull figure, backed up and cheered on by soldiers from all parts of the British empire and commonwealth.

as an institution – and cleared out from Downing Street Horace Wilson, Chamberlain's right-hand man in Whitehall – Churchill worked well with senior permanent officials in the Cabinet Secretariat and his small civil service private-office staff in Number 10. He also set up the Prime Minister's Statistical Section, headed by his personal friend and adviser 'the Prof' (F. A. Lindemann, Lord Cherwell), who was backed up by a small staff, as a sort of personal think-tank, providing analysis and advice, challenging bureaucratic inertia and chasing up decisions.

Churchill was always seeking and using a variety of advice and views, was always determined to make up his own mind, but seldom refused to listen, and was always prepared to weigh a good argument from whatever source it came. At his best, he ranged energetically between geo-politics and grand strategy at one end of the spectrum and sometimes minor administrative details at the other. He made things happen, firing off memoranda and instructions stamped 'Action this Day'. He concentrated on running the war and largely left the 'home front' and domestic policy, and planning for the postwar society and economy, to others. Meetings were carried on often late at night and into the small hours – to the dismay of weary colleagues and generals – and Churchill's methods sometimes wasted a great deal of time. But his staggering capacity for hard work and his ability to absorb, analyse and act on mountains of material was an immense asset. With his constant probing and prodding, he kept others (ministers, generals, officials) up to the mark. Impulsive and amazingly fertile in ideas, he needed ministers, officials and advisers around him to argue him out of the bad or impractical ones and to take the good ones forward. 'Winston produces a hundred ideas a day, of which only six are any good', American President Franklin D. Roosevelt once said.

In personal terms Churchill was a warmer and more genuine human being than any of the other top international leaders and warlords in the Second World War. He was mercurial and experienced great mood swings: according to one aide, 'either on the crest of the wave or in the trough, either highly laudatory or bitterly condemnatory; either in an angelic temper or a hell of a rage'. He was also a sentimentalist and openly exhibited his feelings: 'I blub an awful lot', he once admitted. He could, to be sure, be ruthless

Churchill meeting Franklin D. Roosevelt in 1941. He put tremendous effort into cultivating the American president and into their relationship, which was a vital one but behind the public bonhomie, not straightforward or entirely harmonious.

(when, for instance, he ordered the sinking of French warships to stop them falling into German hands after the fall of France in 1940). But there was also tremendous humanity, magnanimity and unswerving moral decency.

He took the House of Commons immensely seriously during the war, never forgetting that it was a parliamentary revolt that had made him prime minister. Immensely respectful of the traditions of parliament and the constitution, he punctiliously kept MPs informed about the major events and developments of the war, keeping little back – even when the news was bad.

Churchill would, of course, have to be ranked as one of the great political communicators for the powerful and majestic oratory of his famous wartime speeches (mostly made in parliament with some broadcast later on the radio). He had a feel for words and great artistry in their use, but also worked extremely hard at his speechmaking. He mobilized the English language, it was said, and sent it into battle. Some of his phrases are now part of the national vocabulary and the collective historical memory: 'I have nothing to offer but blood, toil, tears and sweat'; 'we shall fight on the beaches, we shall fight on the landing grounds, we shall fight in the fields and in the streets, we shall fight in the hills, we shall never surrender'; 'never in the field of human conflict was so much owed by so many to so few.' He transmitted his resolution to the nation and his showmanship, rhetoric and charisma projected and inspired confidence and determination. However, he never downplayed dangers and setbacks (he admitted Dunkirk was a colossal military disaster, for instance), believing that leaders had to tell the truth wherever possible.

Churchill made a huge personal difference in 1940, at a backs-to-the-wall moment in history, by rallying the nation to continue the war even though it was not easy to see how defeat could be avoided, let alone victory some day secured. If Halifax – or perhaps someone else – had become prime minister, rather than Churchill, it is likely that some sort of peace settlement with Germany would have been negotiated, and the War Cabinet secretly discussed this option. But Churchill strongly rejected the idea, understanding that Hitler's promises and any sort of agreement with him would again be worthless, and believing that Britain and the values it stood for would be finished if it tamely threw in the towel.

For a year after June 1940 Britain faced a Nazi-dominated Europe alone, though with the threat of immediate invasion fading as the Battle of Britain was won. But Churchill knew that the war could not be won without allies. He worked hard at cultivating US President Roosevelt and securing American assistance in the shape of military equipment and supplies that came under the Lend-Lease agreement (though Britain ended up paying heavily for this lifeline). But it was not until the Japanese attack on Pearl Harbor in December 1941 that the US finally came into the war. 'So we had won after all! . . . Many disasters lay ahead, but there was no more doubt about the end', was Churchill's reaction. Earlier, in June 1941 when Germany had invaded Russia, Churchill – hitherto, of course, a consistent opponent of communism – pledged assistance and aid in the common fight against Nazism. 'If Hitler invaded Hell,' he said, 'I would at least make a favourable reference to the Devil in the House of Commons.'

Throughout the war years Churchill put a tremendous effort into the top-level diplomacy of the 'Grand Alliance'. He was the first globe-trotting prime minister, undertaking numerous – often pretty uncomfortable and hazardous – journeys to see things on the spot, make assessments and take decisions, and to negotiate, parley and plan with the other allied leaders and heads of state. He invented the term 'summits' to describe these meetings. He travelled altogether some 150,000 miles (to North America, North Africa and the Middle East, Russia, and elsewhere) at some cost to his health: he was sixty-five years old when he became prime minister, worked punishing hours, and had a heart attack and a near-fatal bout of pneumonia during the war. Relations between the 'Big Three' –

A poster from 1940 showing RAF pilots with Churchill's famous words about the Battle of Britain.

"NEVER WAS SO MUCH OWED BY SO MANY TO SO FEW" THE PRIME MINISTER

Roosevelt, Stalin and Churchill – were in reality often tense and uneasy; they frequently clashed over strategy and the conduct of the war, and ultimately they had divergent national interests and long-term aims. As the war went on Churchill grew increasingly aware that America – whose leadership was hostile to what it saw as British 'colonialism' – was the dominant partner in the 'special relationship'. And he had few illusions about Stalin, becoming gravely concerned about the dominant position the 'Russian Bear' would be left in after the war in Eastern and Central Europe and the Balkans. But the war exposed and exacerbated the great inequalities in national and international power – Britain, Churchill came to realize with dismay, was 'a very *small* country'.

For a long time the war brought little but one grim disaster after another – in Greece, the Mediterranean and North Africa, in the battle against the U-boats in the Atlantic, and in the Far East against Japanese forces. The tide started to turn only at the end of 1942 and in 1943 – after the battle of Stalingrad on the Russian front, and with El Alamein and Anglo-American landings in French North Africa. Churchill was a great champion of a Mediterranean strategy – attacking the enemy's 'soft underbelly', as he told Stalin – leading to the invasion of Sicily after the German/Italian forces had

Churchill was very 'hands on' with the military top brass and with wartime strategy and planning. Here he is in North Africa (1943) conferring with senior British and American generals, including Montgomery and Eisenhower.

Churchill touring the battlefront in France soon after D-Day in 1944.

been expelled from North Africa, and then to the invasion of Italy itself in 1943. The Americans saw Italy and the Balkans as a sideshow, however, and gave priority to the cross-channel invasion of France – something Stalin was always pressing insistently for too. Churchill had great doubts and fears about whether this could succeed, and fought to delay it for as long as he could, operation 'Overlord' finally taking place in June 1944. American military preponderance meant that Churchill's influence over allied strategy continued to decline after 'D-Day' and in the last, hard-fought, year of the war. He got nowhere, for instance, when he urged Roosevelt and General Eisenhower to speed up the advance of British and US forces in order to capture Berlin before the Russians could get to it.

While he recognized that the war would not be won by bombing from 15,000 feet, Churchill had given approval and strong support to the strategic bombing campaign that built up over the war, with large bomber raids on German towns and cities, much destruction and large-scale civilian deaths (as well as frighteningly high rates of loss of allied planes and aircrews). For some time it was about the only way of directly hitting back at Germany. Churchill had occasional misgivings. 'Are we beasts? Are we taking this too far?' he once asked after seeing film of the destruction, but in practice it seems to have had only a limited effect on civilian morale and German war-production. In 1941 Churchill had authorized a top-secret research programme (code-named 'Tube Alloys') that, in conjunction with the Americans, resulted in the development of the atomic bomb. In July 1945 he agreed (without consulting his Cabinet colleagues) to the dropping of atomic bombs on Japan by the Americans without further reference to London (Hiroshima and Nagasaki being bombed in August, after he had left office).

Wary allies: Churchill photographed with Joseph Stalin during the prime minister's visit to Moscow in 1942.

After Germany's surrender in May 1945 Churchill had wanted his coalition government to continue until the defeat of Japan (not then thought to be imminent) but the Labour Party pulled out and for a short time he headed a 'caretaker' government. Parliament was dissolved and the first general election for ten years was held. The unexpected result, announced on 26 July, was a landslide victory for the Labour Party, which won 396 seats in parliament, with the Conservatives reduced to 210 seats. Churchill had not helped matters with a poor campaign and ill-judged broadcasts in which he claimed his erstwhile (and eminently moderate and patriotic) Labour colleagues would have to introduce something like the Gestapo to enforce the rule of totalitarian socialism. The smear backfired. The British people may have cheered Churchill the war leader, but they did not think he would be the right man to deal with the problems of peacetime. During the war he had seemed disengaged from or out of sympathy with the plans for reconstruction and extended welfare provision that were being talked about and drawn up. The public mood had undoubtedly swung to the left. And in a wider sense the 1945 general election was a verdict on the Conservative Party record in the 1930s – the wasted years of the slump and of appeasement. Lloyd George had won his 'khaki election' after his war victory in 1918, but at the moment of his triumph Churchill was rejected and cast out from office. 'It may be a blessing in disguise', Clementine said, hoping to console him. 'At the moment', he grunted, 'it seems quite effectively disguised.'

ELDER STATESMAN

CHURCHILL lived for nearly another twenty years after the war, remaining in frontline politics up until the mid-1950s. He did not enjoy opposition very much after 1945 and was for long periods very much a part-time or absentee Leader of the Opposition. He always liked a good House of Commons ding-dong argument and made grand set piece speeches, but the more pedestrian and uncharismatic Labour premier, Clement Attlee, could often cut him down to size, puncture his rhetorical balloons and score debating victories. He left to others much of the donkeywork of leading the opposition in parliament, overhauling the run-down party organisation, and devising new policies. Conservative recovery after the 1945 defeat happened under Churchill rather than because of him. 'The job of the Leader of the Opposition', he said, was 'to attack the Government – that and no more.' He mounted thunderous attacks on 'socialism', bureaucracy, mismanagement, red tape, queues, shortages, rationing and austerity, and he was often sceptical of the new ideas and initiatives dreamed up by the bright young men of the Conservative Party, but in the end he was willing to make the changes of party policy and image necessary to win.

As ever, Churchill was too much the brilliant individualist to be a good team player or party manager. He often didn't even attend the shadow cabinet, preferring to host fortnightly lunches of the Tory high command at the Savoy – which he called his 'advance battle headquarters' – where large amounts of food and alcohol were consumed and there was as much social as political talk, with the Great Man indulging his love of monologues, afterwards having a nap. It was not surprising that there was an undercurrent of discontent about his leadership in the party, with backbenchers sometimes restive and some frontbenchers muttering that he should bow out. There was no way to force him out but Clementine Churchill would certainly have liked him to retire. He was stunned, shocked and depressed by his sudden and unexpected eviction from power, and exhausted after his gruelling wartime premiership. He was very low at times. But he recovered his spirits, and was determined to fight on, avenge his defeat and be elected in his own right as prime minister.

Opposite:
Churchill in 1951, wearing one of his famous zip-up 'siren suits'.

Bronze bust of Churchill by Oscar Nemon (in the National Portrait Gallery), one of a series resulting from sittings between 1951 and 1953.

The six volumes of his *Second World War* memoirs, that Churchill started working on in 1946, were published between 1948 and 1954. The books were worldwide bestsellers, finally making him a rich man and securing his family's financial future. In 1953 he sealed his reputation as the great statesman-author by winning the Nobel Prize for Literature. Put together with the help of a team of researchers and historians, and even with some behind-the-scenes official assistance, his war memoirs were based on a mass of government documents, minutes and telegrams, with Churchill dictating linking passages and carefully crafting the overall architecture and shape of the argument.

He had once quipped that history would treat him kindly because he would write it. 'This is my case', he said, and the books were a defence of his pre-war stance against appeasement and of his conduct of the war – his version of events, with him centre-stage. They influenced interpretations of the war for years to come. But subsequent historians have shown what he concealed, left out, played down or glossed over. There was no mention, for instance, of the code-breaking triumphs that had supplied him with immensely valuable signals intelligence. He glossed over wartime differences with the Americans and his arguments with the chiefs of staff. Moreover Churchill's war memoirs were not just an account of the recent past as seen from his unique vantage point, and were not just about burnishing his reputation. They were also a way for him to project what he saw as the lessons of the 1930s into the contemporary Cold War context – the need for the West to stand up to the Soviet Union, to keep its defences strong, and for the centrality of Anglo-American unity.

Still a great and commanding international figure, Churchill captured headlines and influenced the agenda of world and European politics after the war with famous speeches – in Fulton, Missouri in 1946, warning about the 'iron curtain' descending across Europe, and in Zurich in 1946, and later in Strasbourg, calling for 'a kind of United States of Europe', built around a new Franco-German 'partnership', and with a democratised Germany fully included in the 'European family'. He even backed the creation of a European army. Churchill has been seen as one of the 'founding fathers' of European unity and he was a leader of the British European movement. But he was certainly not in favour of Britain being part of or swallowed up in a federal Europe. He remained a British nationalist – but not a 'Little Englander'. When he returned to office in 1951 he took the same line as the Attlee government had in ruling out British participation in the Schuman Plan and the European Coal and Steel Community, the institution from which the later EU developed. His warnings about the Russian threat and the need for Western unity and strength against the menace of Soviet communism were initially controversial, but were soon seen as prescient as relations between the West and Stalin's USSR deteriorated. Churchill strongly supported the Truman Doctrine, the Marshall Plan and the creation of NATO that locked the USA into the defence of Western Europe. He coined the term 'special relationship' to describe the alliance with the USA. But Britain, he believed, still had a world role and worldwide interests – a unique role at the centre of what he described as three overlapping circles: Europe, the United States, and the empire/Commonwealth. Not least among the reasons why he stayed in politics was his feeling that he and his country could still play a part and had things to do on the world stage.

Churchill came back into office as prime minister after the October 1951 general election, when the Conservative Party won a majority of seventeen seats in parliament. He was nearly seventy-seven, the oldest prime minister of the twentieth century. The years were clearly taking their toll. His energies were flagging, he was increasingly deaf, and his health was failing. In June 1953 he suffered a serious stroke – concealed from the media and the public – which almost killed him. In 1951 he had given the impression that he would stay in Number 10 for only a year or so but he refused to be prised out of office and kept coming up with excuses to postpone retirement and the end of his political life – something which he dreaded. Although Churchill maintained his public prestige, in private leading ministers and his heir apparent, Anthony Eden, became increasingly uneasy and frustrated. It would be wrong to say that Churchill was 'gaga', and he could still rise to the big occasion, but he was selective in what he did, 'hands-off' in style, and his capacity to direct and lead the government was much reduced compared to his wartime dynamism.

On the domestic front Churchill had no great policy ideas of his own but thought the country needed a period of quiet, steady administration rather than further upheaval and reform. Rationing was ended, house-building was prioritised, the government showed it was anxious to get on with – rather than to take on – the trade unions, there was no attempt to undo the big nationalisations of the Attlee government (with the exception of the steel industry and road haulage), and care was taken to show the welfare state was safe in Tory hands. Churchill presided benignly over a middle-of-the-road government. Later critics, with the benefit of hindsight, argued that a tougher free-market and modernising stance should have been adopted and that Britain

A Graham Sutherland study of Churchill (1954). Sutherland's controversial portrait of Churchill, presented to him by the two Houses of Parliament to celebrate his eightieth birthday, was violently disliked by Winston and Clementine and later destroyed on the latter's instructions.

Churchill being invested as a Knight of the Garter at Windsor Castle, June 1954.

started to lose ground in this period compared to its economic rivals. But at the time, the government seemed competent, moderate and relatively successful. The accession and coronation of the young Queen Elizabeth II stirred the old statesman and appealed to his sense of the drama, romance and pageantry of monarchy and empire – sentiments that still had popular purchase in the early 1950s. The Queen made him a Knight of the Garter in 1953 and he finally became 'Sir Winston'.

Churchill's primary personal interests and his great ambitions for his second premiership lay in foreign affairs. He wanted to revive and strengthen the wartime 'special relationship' with the USA, and launched a one-man campaign for a high-level summit meeting with the Americans and the Russians to try to defuse Cold War tensions. Britain was still a great power, he believed, and the government decided in 1954 to build the hydrogen bomb. But Churchill saw his last great role as being that of international peacemaker and he felt deeply the need to do all he could to avert the danger of a nuclear holocaust. The Americans were personally welcoming, and Churchill visited Truman and then Eisenhower in the White House. But the view in Washington DC was that Churchill was trying to re-live the glory days of the Second World War 'Big Three' and that his outlook and plans took no account of the new realities of power. Half American as he was, Churchill over-sentimentalised the Anglo-American relationship and over-estimated the influence he and Britain could have on US policymakers. The Russians rebuffed him too and in the end nothing came of his plans.

Churchill celebrated his eightieth birthday in 1954. He once said that he always believed in staying in the pub until closing time and he had clung on tenaciously to office far longer than anyone expected – privately doubtful that his chosen successor, Anthony Eden, was really up to the job of being prime minister – until, accepting he was too old to lead the Conservatives into another general election, he left reluctantly and under intense pressure from his political colleagues in April 1955. The Queen offered him a dukedom but he was proud to be the 'Great Commoner' and had no desire to sit in the House of Lords, remaining an MP in the House of Commons – an institution where he had spent most of his life. From time to time he attended sessions but he did not speak in parliament again and visited his constituency only rarely. There was talk that, uniquely, he be made an honorary Life Member of Parliament, but the government turned down the idea. Only in the last year of his life, in 1964, did he finally leave the House of Commons.

A sense of political failure and disappointment took hold of him. He was dismayed by the Suez debacle that destroyed Eden's premiership. 'I would never have done it without squaring the Americans', he said of the abortive military intervention in 1956 against Egypt's Nasser, 'and once I'd started I would never have dared stop.' He lamented what he called the 'woe and ruin of the terrible twentieth century.' 'We answered all the tests', he said, 'but it was useless.' All that Churchill had stood for and fought for he felt had been lost or was passing away, and he came to feel he had achieved nothing, and that Britain's power and empire were fast declining.

Aided by a team of historians and aides, he completed his four-volume *History of the English-Speaking Peoples*, originally begun before the Second

Churchill and the Cabinet photographed in 1955 before the announcement of his retirement. Aged eighty, Churchill was reluctant to go but his frustrated colleagues were privately relieved at his departure.

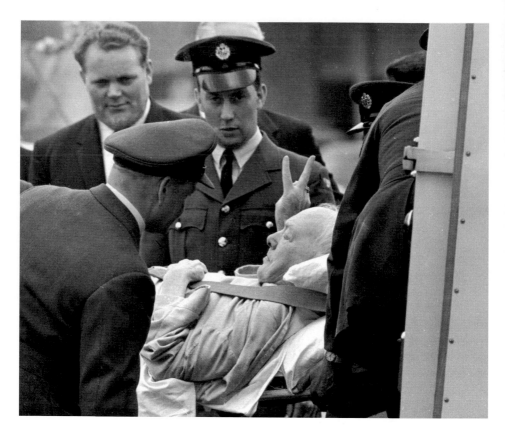

Churchill giving his famous 'V' sign as he is stretchered away and flown to hospital after breaking his thigh in France in 1962.

World War. It sold well chiefly because of the fame of its author, but had a decidedly old-fashioned feel to it, with its narrative of kings, battles and constitutional struggles. Influenced by his scientist friend, Lord Cherwell, he led a financial appeal to create a British equivalent of America's scientific and technological powerhouse MIT, the outcome being the establishment of a new Cambridge college, named after him.

'I have got to kill time till time kills me', was Churchill's bitter comment about his retirement. It was a bleak and melancholy decline, a process of physical decay and increasing illness, and clouded by depression (his 'black dog'), lethargy and infirmity. A visitor in the later 1950s likened him to 'the embers of a great fire – all the force is gone'. He spent much time abroad, chiefly in the south of France, attracted as always by the warmth, light and colours of the Riviera, or cruising in the Mediterranean or the West Indies on the yacht of the Greek ship-owner Aristotle Onassis.

Family problems crowded in. Clementine Churchill was often in poor health herself; relations with his son Randolph had long been difficult, even

Churchill's funeral parade outside St Paul's Cathedral, London, in 1965.

tempestuous, though he approved his appointment as official biographer; one daughter, Sarah, had serious drink problems, while another, Diana, committed suicide in 1963. His youngest and favourite daughter, Mary, had married Christopher Soames, who became a Conservative MP and minister.

Churchill turned ninety in November 1964. In January 1965 he suffered a massive stroke and after lingering in a coma for two weeks, while crowds thronged the street outside his London home, died on 24 January (exactly seventy years to the day after the death of his father). He was given a magnificent and carefully stage-managed state funeral, with a lying-in-state in Westminster Hall, a military procession through central London with his coffin on a flag-draped gun carriage, and a funeral service at St Paul's Cathedral. Churchill was buried next to the graves of his father, mother and brother in Bladon Churchyard near to his birthplace at Blenheim Palace.

FURTHER READING

Addison, Paul. *Churchill on the Home Front*. Pimlico, 1993.

Addison, Paul. *Churchill*. Oxford University Press, 2005.

Best, Geoffrey. *Churchill: A Study in Greatness*. Hambledon and London, 2001.

Blake, Robert and Louis, W. Roger (eds). *Churchill*. Oxford University Press, 1993.

Churchill, Randolph. *Winston S. Churchill, Vol. I: Youth*. Heinemann, 1966.

Churchill, Randolph. *Winston S. Churchill, Vol. II: Young Statesman*. Heinemann, 1967.

Colville, John. *The Fringes of Power*. Hodder and Stoughton, 1985.

Gilbert, Martin. *Winston S. Churchill, Vol. III: The Challenge of War*. Heinemann, 1971.

Gilbert, Martin. *Winston S. Churchill, Vol. IV: A Stricken World*. Heinemann, 1975.

Gilbert, Martin. *Winston S. Churchill, Vol. V: Prophet of Truth*. Heinemann, 1976.

Gilbert, Martin. *Winston S. Churchill, Vol. VI: Finest Hour*. Heinemann, 1983.

Gilbert, Martin. *Winston S. Churchill, Vol. VII: The Road to Victory*. Heinemann, 1986.

Gilbert, Martin. *Winston S. Churchill, Vol. VIII: Never Despair*. Heinemann, 1988.

Hastings, Max. *Finest Years: Churchill as Warlord 1940–45*. HarperPress, 2009.

James, Robert Rhodes. *Churchill: A Study in Failure*. Weidenfeld and Nicolson, 1970.

Jenkins, Roy. *Churchill*. Macmillan, 2001.

Moran, Lord. *Winston Churchill: The Struggle for Survival, 1940–55*. Constable, 1966.

Ramsden, John. *Churchill: Man of the Century*. HarperCollins, 2002.

Reynolds, David. In Command of History: *Churchill Fighting and Writing the Second World War*. Penguin, 2004.

Soames, Mary. *Clementine Churchill*. Cassell, 1979.

Taylor, A. J. P. et al. *Churchill: Four Faces and the Man*. Allen Lane, 1969.

Toye, Richard. *Churchill's Empire*. Macmillan, 2010.

The papers of Sir Winston Churchill, and other archives documenting the Churchill era, are held at Churchill College in Cambridge (www.chu.cam.ac.uk/archives).

PLACES TO VISIT
ASSOCIATED WITH CHURCHILL

BLENHEIM PALACE
Built between 1705 and 1722, Blenheim Palace was a gift from the nation to John Churchill, the first Duke of Marlborough, after his military triumphs against the French King Louis XIV. One of the grandest houses in England, it was designed by Vanbrugh in the English Baroque style and its grounds were later laid out by 'Capability' Brown. It was never Winston Churchill's home, though he was born there, visited and stayed often, and proposed to his wife in its gardens (at the Temple of Diana, overlooking the lake). Blenheim Palace is located in the village of Woodstock, eight miles from Oxford (website: www.blenheimpalace.com). Churchill was buried in 1965 in the churchyard at Bladon, close to Blenheim.

CHARTWELL
Bought in 1922 by Churchill for its magnificent views over the Weald of Kent, Chartwell, near Westerham in Kent, and only 24 miles from Westminster, was his home and the place from which he drew inspiration from 1924 until the end of his life. During the Second World War the house was mostly unused, considered as potentially vulnerable to a German airstrike or commando-style raid; the Churchills instead spent their weekends at Ditchley Park in Oxfordshire or at the prime minister's official country residence at Chequers. In 1946 a consortium of wealthy businessmen purchased Chartwell and presented it to the National Trust on condition that, for a nominal rent, Churchill would continue to live there and that after his death it would be opened to the public. The rooms at Chartwell, rich in memorabilia, remain much as they were when Churchill lived there. Many of his paintings can be seen in the studio there. The grounds reflect Churchill's love of the landscape and nature, and include the lakes he created and the water garden where he fed his fish. (Chartwell, Mapleton Road, Westerham, Kent TN16 1PS. Telephone: 01732 868381. Website: www.nationaltrust.org.uk/main/w-chartwell).

CHURCHILL WAR ROOMS
This branch of the Imperial War Museum consists of the Cabinet War Rooms and the Churchill Museum. Visitors can tour the cramped underground headquarters complex in Whitehall where ministers, top officials and military advisers worked and slept during the Second World War. Highlights include the Map Room, the Cabinet Room, the Transatlantic Telephone Room (where Churchill could speak on a secure line to President Roosevelt) and Churchill's own office-bedroom (though he only rarely slept there, preferring to sleep at 10 Downing Street or the No. 10 Annexe, a flat in the New Public Offices directly above the Cabinet War Rooms). The Churchill Museum tells the story of Churchill's life. (Churchill War Rooms, Clive Steps, King Charles Street, London SW1A 2AQ. Website: cwr.iwm.org.uk). The story of the building and use of the Cabinet War Rooms is told in *Churchill's Bunker* by Richard Holmes (Profile Books, 2009).

INDEX